THE

ABCs
OF
SELF
LOVE

A SIMPLE GUIDE TO LOVING YOURSELF,
RECLAIMING YOUR WORTH, AND CHANGING YOUR LIFE

MELODY GODFRED
THE SELF LOVE PHILOSOPHER

Andrews McMeel
PUBLISHING®

Andrews McMeel Publishing
a division of Andrews McMeel Universal
1130 Walnut Street, Kansas City, Missouri 64106

www.andrewsmcmeel.com

22 23 24 25 26 VEP 10 9 8 7 6 5 4 3 2 1

ISBN: 978-1-5248-7123-9

Library of Congress Control Number: 2021943265

Editor: Patty Rice
Art Director: Julie Barnes
Designer: Leanne Aranador
Production Editors: Elizabeth A. Garcia and Thea Voutiritsas
Production Manager: Cliff Koehler

ATTENTION: SCHOOLS AND BUSINESSES
Andrews McMeel books are available at quantity discounts with bulk purchase for educational, business, or sales promotional use. For information, please e-mail the Andrews McMeel Publishing Special Sales Department: specialsales@amuniversal.com.

DEDICATION

This book is dedicated to your true self.

SO MANY YEARS
OF EDUCATION
YET NOBODY
EVER TAUGHT US
HOW TO LOVE
OURSELVES
AND WHY IT'S
SO IMPORTANT.

—UNKNOWN

OF ALL THE THINGS I'VE EVER LEARNED, LOVING MYSELF CHANGED THINGS THE MOST.

I wrote this guide to transform self love from an ambiguous goal into a daily practice. You can commit to reading one letter a day or week or you can read through the entire book in one sitting. You can go through it sequentially or use it as an oracle: open up to random pages to receive the message you need.

Remember: through this book, the gift you are giving to yourself is YOU. Enjoy the journey.

With love,
MELODY GODFRED

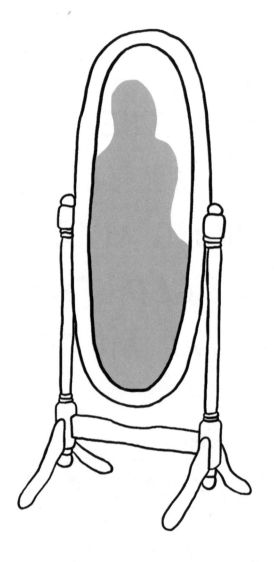

WHEN YOU CAN STAND NAKED
BEFORE YOURSELF,
STRIPPED OF GUILT AND SHAME,
EXPECTATIONS AND REGRETS,
THE PERSON YOU WILL SEE BEFORE YOU
IS YOUR AUTHENTIC SELF.

AUTHENTICITY

A: AUTHENTICITY

To love yourself, you must first know yourself, which is why authenticity is so critical. When we're born, we are the truest version of ourselves. As we grow up, we accumulate a layer of dust: the dust of expectations, of responsibilities, of conformity, of trauma, of pain. This dust dulls our essence, our most authentic selves.

Take a moment to think back to your childhood self. That authentic, dust-free version who made choices from a place of love instead of fear, and instinct instead of learned behaviors. Once you discover that authentic self, imagine abandoning the dust, the stories, the self-imposed limiting behaviors and thoughts that have kept your authentic self hidden.

That person you're envisioning right now? That's your ME. It's time to let your ME lead again.

And if it is painful for you to connect to your childhood, honor who you are today: because your resilience is proof that your authentic self is powerful beyond measure and your ME is ready to shine.

SELF LOVE
IN ACTION

Find a picture from your childhood (or from today if you don't want to revisit your childhood), and use it as the home screen image on your phone. When you see it, reconnect with your most authentic self. Remember who you are, beneath the dust of shame, guilt, pain, regret, and fear.

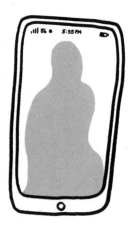

As you go through your day, ask yourself: What would my ME do?

Write a bit about what happens when you let your ME lead:

_____

_____

_____

_____

_____

_____

_____

_____

_____

_____

_____

_____

BOUNDARIES

AREN'T ABOUT WHAT YOU SAY NO TO. THEY'RE ABOUT WHAT YOU MAKE

SPACE FOR.

BOUNDARIES

B: BOUNDARIES

Boundaries aren't just about drawing a line. They are about knowing yourself well enough to know where to draw the line, and having the confidence and self worth to honor it. No two people have the same needs. A boundary ensures that both you and the people in your life know what your needs are so you can both honor them. Not sure if someone has crossed one of your boundaries? Check in with your body. When something happens and in response you feel off, chances are a boundary was crossed.

Since your needs are constantly evolving, no boundary is ever absolute. You have to consistently check in with yourself and see if the boundary is still accurate. In order for a boundary to exist in the world, you must communicate it, which takes vulnerability. If you're anything like me, confrontation is highly uncomfortable. Communicating a boundary may require a small confrontation, but having a boundary is what alleviates the need for big confrontations down the road. Setting a boundary can be intimidating, but ultimately, it is both exhilarating and freeing. The first time you set one, communicate it, and stick to it, you'll see.

SELF LOVE
IN ACTION

Practice setting boundaries. For each category, set a boundary and then communicate it: friends, family, love, work, play. Keep in mind: boundaries aren't just about saying no; they're also about saying yes!

Here are some examples:
Friends: No engaging with negative or toxic people
Family: No saying yes purely out of obligation
Love: No important conversations via text
Work: No checking work emails after 7 p.m.
Play: Yes to fun experiences with people I enjoy

Your turn:

FRIENDS: _____

_____

_____

FAMILY: _____

_____

_____

LOVE: _____

_____

_____

WORK: _____

_____

_____

PLAY: _____

_____

Now that you have set some boundaries, write about how your life has changed.

_____

_____

_____

_____

_____

_____

_____

_____

_____

_____

_____

_____

_____

_____

_____

_____

_____

_____

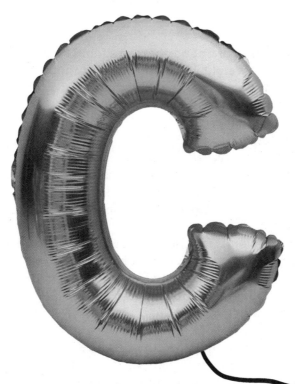

THE FOUR C'S:
CLARITY
COMMITMENT
CREATION
COMMUNITY

C: THE FOUR C'S
CLARITY, COMMITMENT, CREATION & COMMUNITY

When choosing a diamond, there are four C's: cut, clarity, color, and carat weight. When it comes to choosing yourself, there are four C's, as well, that together embody your self love journey.

The first C stands for clarity, which represents getting to know your authentic self, needs, wants, and goals. Clarity is the pathway to intentional living. It makes your happiness something that isn't coincidental or fleeting but rather a gift you give yourself by knowing and honoring yourself.

The second C stands for commitment, which represents committing to daily practices that honor your true self and nurture your mind and body. Commitment is what transforms your clarity into manifestation, thoughts into action, dreams into waking life.

The third C is creation (magic!), which is what you manifest when you love and choose yourself daily. Creation is what happens when clarity and commitment come into alignment. You unlock parts of yourself you didn't even know existed—perhaps even the best parts.

The fourth C is community, which is what you will cultivate around you to support and celebrate your commitment to yourself, your clarity, your creations. Because self love is not a solo expedition—exactly the opposite. When you move through the world from a place of self love and worth, you seek out human connection with others who are also on a similar journey. You choose yourselves and, as a result, are whole enough to deeply connect with each other.

SELF LOVE
IN ACTION

For the next four days, pick one of the four C's to focus on.

DAY ONE - CLARITY:

Spend fifteen minutes first thing in the morning
journaling in response to these prompts:

I AM

I NEED

I WANT

I BELIEVE

I KNOW

I CAN

I WILL

DAY TWO - COMMITMENT:

Devote at least one hour today to honoring the discoveries you made yesterday about who you are by engaging in some self care. Do something that is just for you. Write down what you did, and share how you felt afterward:

DAY THREE - CREATION:

Channel your inner creator by doing something that isn't about productivity but instead is about feeding your soul and nurturing your inner creative. What did you create?

DAY FOUR - COMMUNITY:

Plan a night with friends to make vision boards to empower
your self love journeys. Write down what you want your
board to focus on, and include the date you set
for the vision board session:

DAY FIVE:
Reflect on how you feel today compared
with how you felt on day one:

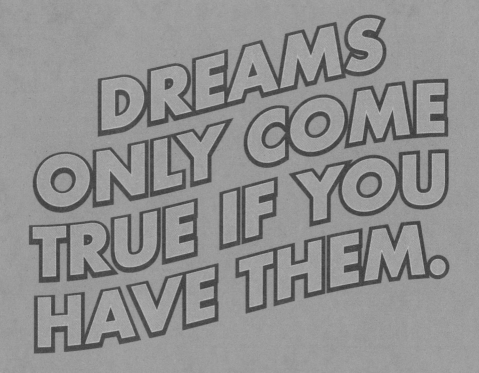

DAILY DREAM

D: DAILY DREAM

Chances are you have a to-do list, whether it's written down in a notebook, exists digitally on your phone and computer, or is simply a mental load you struggle to keep up with. The question is, when you review that list, what percentage of it relates to soul-sucking aspects of your day (i.e., paying bills), as opposed to soul-filling ones (i.e., dreaming)?

Until recently, dreaming wasn't on my list. And as a result, my spirit was slowly succumbing to the responsibilities of my everyday life. That's when dreaming came in and changed everything. A friend and I set a calendar alert called DAILY DREAM for 5 p.m. every day. When it goes off, we spend fifteen minutes dreaming, and then we text each other about it. Once we started creating space to dream, our dreams started coming true. Not all of them, and not all at once, but as we became more intentional about dreaming, we were able to transform our lives into lives worth dreaming about.

On May 21, 2018, this was my daily dream: "I dream of being on a beach. Warm water. White sand. Music. My favorite people. A cold drink. No Internet." By 2021, I had forgotten about my dream. But it hadn't forgotten about me: On May 21, 2021, I landed in Miami, and soon found myself on the beach, living the precise moment I had dreamed about. The best part? My dream partner's May 21, 2018, dream came true at exactly the same time as mine: she finally moved to a new home that included her very own washer and dryer. Three years later—our dreams came true—together.

SELF LOVE
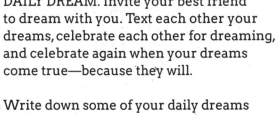
IN ACTION

Set a calendar alert that repeats called
DAILY DREAM. Invite your best friend
to dream with you. Text each other your
dreams, celebrate each other for dreaming,
and celebrate again when your dreams
come true—because they will.

Write down some of your daily dreams
and don't forget to write their dates:

ALL THE WAYS WE
TRY TO AVOID OUR
PAIN WHEN THE
ONLY WAY THROUGH
IS TO FEEL IT.

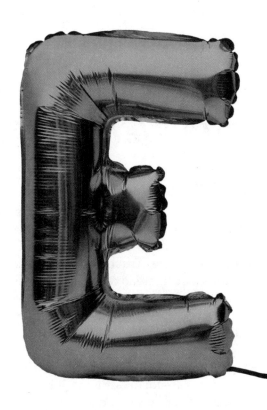

EMOTIONAL
EMPOWERMENT

E: EMOTIONAL EMPOWERMENT

Two of the phrases we hear most often as babies and children are "Don't cry" and "You're okay." And so we're raised to believe that painful feelings shouldn't be expressed or felt. We all know what follows—a lifetime of buried feelings like shame, guilt, pain, anger, frustration, and sadness—that isolate and debilitate us. Instead of feeling our "unapproved" feelings and allowing them to show us the root causes of our discomfort, we do everything we can to avoid them. We carry them around like our shadows.

Emotional empowerment is about feeling all of our emotions and inviting them to transform our lives. It is about practicing complete self acceptance so that no feeling is off limits. Once we feel what needs to be felt, we can decide how we want to think and act next. Think of your feelings as a teacher instead of a burden, and let feeling everything become as natural as breathing. Because once you feel, you can explore, release, and move on, and motion is the root of life, growth, and, of course, self love.

SELF LOVE
IN ACTION

Spend the day feeling your feelings and getting curious about them. As emotions come up, create space for them (instead of burying or judging them), and then ask yourself, "How come?" Follow the "how comes" until you get to the root issue. If you're not happy with the cause of your feelings, see if there's anything you can do to change it. If not, see how you can shift your perspective to create peace of mind and acceptance within yourself and with your world.

FEELING: _____

HOW COME? _____

_____

_____

_____

FEELING: _____

HOW COME? _____

_____

_____

_____

FEELING: _____

HOW COME? _____

_____

_____

_____

_____

Sometimes all it takes to feel better is to get out of your mind and onto the page. Pick one feeling that you identified above and explore it further:

forgive.
not because
they deserve it,
but because
you do.

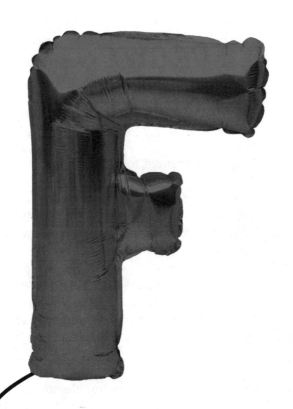

FORGIVENESS
(FREEDOM)

F: FORGIVENESS (FREEDOM)

Want to feel truly free? Forgive, forgive, forgive.

The root of "forgive" comes from the Latin word *perdonare*, which means "to pardon; to give completely, without reservation." This is the kind of forgiveness you owe not just to those who have hurt you but also to yourself.

What makes forgiveness unique is that it is a gift both to the recipient and to the giver. Until you forgive, you remain stuck in the wrongdoing that harmed you (which only escalates your pain). Forgive. Not because they deserve it but because you do.

Forgiveness is what allows you to unshackle yourself from the past so you can live in the present and dream into the future. While your ego may push you to carry a grudge, remember that your ego isn't your true self. Your ego cares about right and wrong, blame and shame. Your true self craves joy, magic, lightness, and peace. To honor your true self, it's important not just to forgive others but also to forgive yourself, freely, fully, quickly, completely, and without reservation. Because once you do, you'll free your authentic self to create, to love, to heal, and to live unencumbered by the mistakes of the past.

SELF LOVE
IN ACTION

Write a letter of forgiveness to someone who has wronged you, and write another one to yourself. Whether you share the letters is secondary. The freedom comes from feeling them.

FORGIVENESS LETTER TO: ME

_____

_____

_____

_____

_____

_____

_____

_____

_____

_____

_____

_____

_____

_____

_____

_____

FORGIVENESS LETTER TO:_____

_____

_____

_____

_____

_____

_____

_____

_____

_____

_____

_____

_____

_____

_____

_____

_____

_____

_____

_____

_____

_____

_____

_____

_____

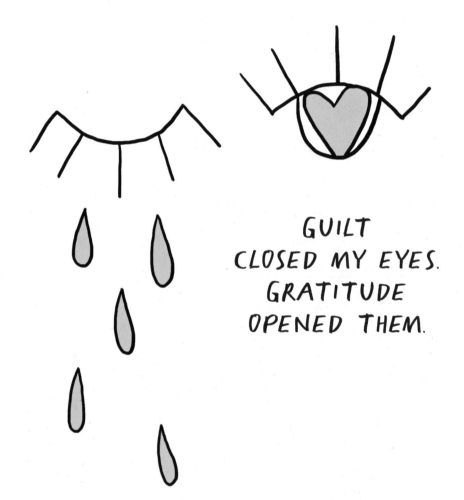

GUILT
CLOSED MY EYES.
GRATITUDE
OPENED THEM.

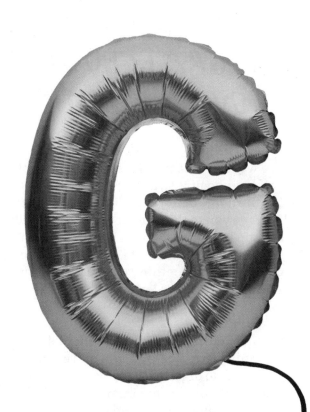

GRATITUDE
OVER GUILT

G: GRATITUDE OVER GUILT

Gratitude is a word you hear quite a bit once you start exploring self love, positivity, and mindfulness. While the traditional definition—being thankful—is important, I'm going to challenge you to think of gratitude a little differently. For me, gratitude isn't just about being thankful. It is about being truly present in the moment I'm experiencing, instead of feeling guilty about something outside of my current experience. Gratitude is how I love and choose myself—without apology.

Let me explain. If you're a working parent like I am, you spend a lot of time feeling guilty that you're not with your kids, instead of feeling grateful that you're at work (and vice versa). The moment I flipped my internal switch from guilt to gratitude, my happiness increased exponentially. And this doesn't just apply to real-time conflicts. Oftentimes, it's the guilt from the past or guilt about something in the future that takes the joy out of a present experience—that takes us out of our present experience.

Guilt robs you of the moment you're in. Gratitude reclaims it. When we focus on the moment we're in and practice gratitude instead of guilt, we ground ourselves (and especially our runaway thoughts) in joy. And joy is what lights the way on our self love journeys.

IN ACTION

SENSORY GRATITUDE EXERCISE

This grounding meditation is designed to use your sensory experience to ground you not just in the present moment but also in gratitude. Always remember that when your mind is running away from you, your body is the key to finding your way back home.

Find a quiet space, preferably outside, and sit in a comfortable position. Close your eyes. For each of your senses, with your sight being the last, express something you're grateful for in this very moment and place:

TOUCH:

_____

_____

_____

_____

_____

_____

_____

_____

_____

_____

_____

_____

SMELL:

SOUND:

TASTE:

_____

_____

_____

_____

_____

_____

_____

_____

SIGHT:

_____

_____

_____

_____

_____

_____

_____

_____

Now that you're here, be here. Don't let guilt, shame, regret, anger, or fear take over the precious gift of life you're experiencing right now.

NEGATIVE THOUGHT:

I BELIEVED IT SO DEEPLY
IT BECAME REAL.

POSITIVE THOUGHT:

I BELIEVED IT SO DEEPLY
IT BECAME REAL.

YOUR CHOICE.

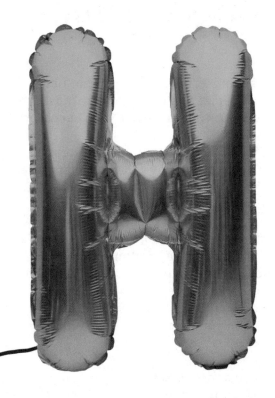

HAPPY THOUGHTS

H: HAPPY THOUGHTS

It took me reaching an emotional rock bottom to finally seek the help of a therapist. She taught me the most extraordinary truth: just like I can choose myself, I can choose my thoughts.

As someone who naturally assumes the worst, learning that I can bend my thoughts to my will changed my life. Imagine you're a surfer and you're sitting on your board in the middle of the ocean waiting for a wave. You see a huge monster of a wave approaching that is certain to bury you. In that moment, you can choose: do I want to get on this wave, or do I want to wait for the next one? Now, when something happens and I feel a negative reaction coming on, I pause and let that monster wave pass me by. I choose to wait for a nug (surfer slang for a good wave) instead. It requires mindfulness and patience, which both require work, but it's worth it.

Let me give you another example: I send my friend a text, and she doesn't immediately respond. My old fearful self would immediately assume, "Oh no. I did something wrong. She's mad at me." Now, when that thought presents itself (because it still does), I choose a happy thought instead. "Oh, she is busy. She'll get back to me later."

And that happy thought is the right one 99.9 percent of the time.

Regardless of the circumstances you're facing, how you think about them is truly 100 percent up to you. Choose a positive perspective, choose the happy thoughts, get on the happy wave, and enjoy the ride.

SELF LOVE
IN ACTION

Create a Happy Thoughts playlist to serve as your reset trigger when happy thoughts feel hard to come by. When negative thoughts dominate your mental ocean, listen to your playlist to slow down your mind, and then try to see the situation you're facing from a different, more positive perspective.

HAPPY THOUGHTS PLAYLIST:

"HAPPY"-PHARRELL

"LOVELY DAY"-BILL WITHERS

"SOULMATE"-LIZZO

"LOVE ON TOP"-BEYONCÉ

"BIRD SET FREE"-SIA

"GOLDEN"-JILL SCOTT

"BACK IN MY BODY"-MAGGIE ROGERS

"TREAT MYSELF"-MEGHAN TRAINOR

"I'M STILL STANDING"-ELTON JOHN

"HIGHER LOVE"-KYGO & WHITNEY HOUSTON

"REACH OUT I'LL BE THERE"-FOUR TOPS

"FREEDOM! '90"-GEORGE MICHAEL

"DANCING IN THE MOONLIGHT"-TOPLOADER

"DON'T YOU WORRY 'BOUT A THING"-STEVIE WONDER
(OR TORI KELLY, BECAUSE I LOVE A COVER)

MY HAPPY THOUGHTS PLAYLIST:

1. _____

2. _____

3. _____

4. _____

5. _____

6. _____

7. _____

8. _____

9. _____

10. _____

11. _____

12. _____

13. _____

14. _____

15. _____

Write about how your perspective shifted after listening to your
Happy Thoughts playlist:

MY
INTUITION
CREATES
SPACE
FOR THE
UNKNOWN.
IT CAN
REMEMBER
THE PAST
WITHOUT BEING
DEFINED BY IT.
IT CAN MANIFEST
THE FUTURE
WITHOUT BEING
TIED TO IT.
IT IS PRESENT.
IT IS PEACEFUL.
IT IS POWERFUL.

INTUITION

I: INTUITION

You know that funny "knowing" feeling you get sometimes, the one deep down in the pit of your stomach or on the edges of your mind? The one that signals something to you without you knowing exactly how or why? Meet your intuition. The angel you didn't know you had.

The beauty of intuition is that it is inherent, not learned, and doesn't need any facts or justification to make its case. It's there for you, watching out for you, all the time. The problem is that, in most cases, we're simply too busy, distracted, or skeptical to recognize or hear it. Your intuition is the voice of your true, authentic self, your ME, the part of you that is tapped into the universe. Your intuition doesn't think—it KNOWS. Once you start making space for it, your intuition will become impossible to miss. It will reach for you through your other senses, as well, so pay attention to bodily cues. Once you feel connected to your intuition, the next step is to start setting intentions.

Use your intuition as guidance and become intentional about how you live your life. Make choices that align with and honor your authentic self. Because once your intentions are aligned with your intuition, your life will change into one that resonates with you on a mind, body, and soul level.

SELF LOVE
IN ACTION

Create space so your intuition can speak up. Allocate five minutes each morning and five minutes before bed to meditate and free your mind of the clutter that drowns out your intuition. Find a comfortable spot, sit in a resting position, and let your mind and body slowly relax into a place of being instead of doing. Breathe in for five counts; breathe out for ten.

If you have trouble quieting your mind, use a mantra to center yourself, or engage in a repetitive (nondigital) movement like playing scales on an instrument, weeding your garden, going for a run, or taking a shower.

Now listen—not just to your mind but also to your body—for cues and guidance. What did you discover?

Another space where you can listen for your intuition is in your dreams. Keep an intuition diary, and write down the things your intuition shows and tells you in both your waking life and your dream life. Once you start paying attention, you'll realize it talks to you and helps you all the time. Extra points if you start tracking moments when your intuition guided you to a divine, "meant to be" outcome.

MY INTUITION DIARY:

SOMETIMES I'M A HAPPY RAY OF SUNSHINE.

SOMETIMES I'M A MELANCHOLY BEAM OF MOONLIGHT.

HAPPY OR SAD, I AM STILL WHOLE.

I AM STILL WORTHY.

I AM STILL ENOUGH.

I AM STILL GRATEFUL.

I AM STILL JOYFUL.

I AM STILL ME.

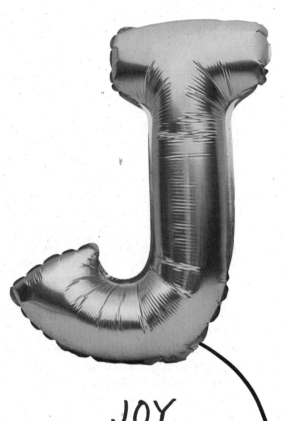

JOY

J: JOY

While the terms "happiness" and "joy" are oftentimes used interchangeably, they are actually two distinct pieces of the self love equation that work together.

Whereas happiness is a state of mind that comes in response to external experiences, joy is a more constant, internal state of being. For example: happiness is when you start getting paid for your creative work; joy is knowing your art is worthy of an audience regardless. One is externally triggered; the other is deeply connected to your internal sense of worth, peace, and wellness. While happiness is important, joy is critical—as only joy will sustain you through whatever highs and lows life presents.

When it comes to self love, we talk a lot about embracing and experiencing your darkest feelings. But according to Dr. Brené Brown, it takes just as much courage (if not more!) to experience your joy as it does to embrace your sorrow. "Joy is the most vulnerable emotion we experience," Brown says. "And if you cannot tolerate joy, what you do is you start dress rehearsing tragedy." Dress rehearsing tragedy is when you disclaim your joy by preparing yourself for the worst (which is sure to follow . . . or is it?).

Joy is a state of being that requires nurture in the form of gratitude and trust. It also requires that you get very comfortable with uncertainty because the circumstances both within you and external to you can change. So when you feel the warm glow of joy radiate from within, really feel it, and let it carry you through everything that follows.

SELF LOVE
IN ACTION

Sometimes the joy within us becomes
dormant due to the weight of our
routines. To wake up your joy, shake
up your rituals. Commit to one week
of new everything: a new shampoo or
soap to change the scent in your shower,
a new breakfast, a new route to work,
new music, a new workout class, a new
bar/restaurant/museum for after work.
Make plans with a new friend. Take a last-
minute day trip. Change up your going-
to-bed ritual. Shop for a little something
new for yourself.

At the end of the week, all the newness should wake up the spark of
joy within you. From there, use gratitude to nurture it, and make the
new things that worked part of your weekly rituals.

NEWNESS LIST
Write down the new things you tried and loved:

CERTIFICATE OF
AUTHENTICITY

_____

YOUR NAME

IS ONE OF A KIND

YOU ARE THE ONLY YOU
WHO WILL EVER EXIST.
ONE OF ONE,
WITHOUT A SINGLE REPLICA,
PAST, PRESENT, OR FUTURE.

THIS IS NO ACCIDENT.

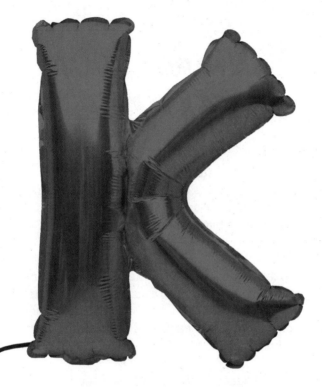

KNOW YOUR
NARRATIVE

K: KNOW YOUR NARRATIVE

To love yourself, know and own your narrative. Your narrative is your story. It is the unique blend of inherent magic and earned experience that makes you uniquely you. It is what allows you to leave an imprint on the world in a way no one else can.

Once we realize the power that comes with being one in nearly eight billion, we can start reclaiming all parts of ourselves and our stories instead of segregating ourselves into "good" parts and "bad" parts and disclaiming the "bad" parts of ourselves and our stories.

What once was a source of shame is now a source of strength. What once was a series of disconnected events and outcomes is now the one-of-a-kind formula that belongs only to you. Instead of seeing yourself as a series of circumstantial events and characteristics, see the through line: the you that connects it all.

Know your narrative and embrace it with pride.
Because yours is the story of a lifetime.

SELF LOVE
IN ACTION

Write a few lines for every year of your life. Write the year in big block letters at the top of each line and your age at the time, and then dive into your mental, emotional, and physical memory. Write about what happened and how you felt. Once you're done, see if you can identify some common themes. What is the through line? What is your purpose? Why are you here?

Use this as an opportunity to revisit and heal old wounds and to forgive yourself and others for any events that caused you to lose sight of your authentic self, power, and magic.

Because it's never too late to heal—never.

YEAR / AGE:

_____

_____

_____

_____

_____

_____

_____

_____

_____

_____

_____

_____

_____

_____

Need more room? There are extra pages for you at the end of this book.

I WORRIED MYSELF INTO THE DARKNESS. I LOVED MYSELF INTO THE LIGHT.

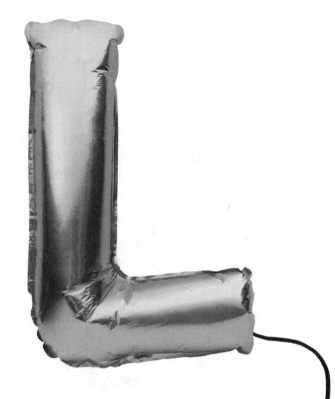

LIGHT

L: LIGHT

The definition of the word "light" is one of my favorites.
The word encompasses so many unique definitions,
and yet they play into each other so gracefully. Light is what
stimulates sight and makes things visible. Light is brilliance.
Illumination. To see the light is to become enlightened—to
unravel a mystery. To be a light is to be a leader, a luminary,
an expert. Lightness is simplicity. Ease. Gentleness.
Weightlessness. Freedom from worry. Freedom itself.

Your inner light is what makes you, you. When ignited,
it makes you feel the most alive—and most free.
Understanding your light and nurturing it is how you
discover your purpose and build a life in alignment with
your true, authentic self. In short—practicing self love is
what illuminates your entire world with the flame of one
match: you.

So be light. In its myriad of definitions. Be the light that
illuminates the world. Shed the weight of uncertainty, risk,
anger, resentment, doubt, guilt, and shame, and be light.
Unravel the mystery of yourself, and let your inner light set
your soul on fire. Be light, be light, be light.

SELF LOVE
IN ACTION

Use the power of a flame as your symbol of self illumination and empowerment. Light a candle every night for a week, and as you watch the flame, imagine it is your own inner light flickering. Go within yourself and discover what your light needs so you can feel light, give light, be light.

Write about your light:

MY LIGHT IS

WHEN I CAN'T MOVE MY MIND, I MOVE MY BODY.

WHEN I CAN'T MOVE MY BODY, I MOVE MY MIND. EITHER WAY—MOVEMENT HEALS.

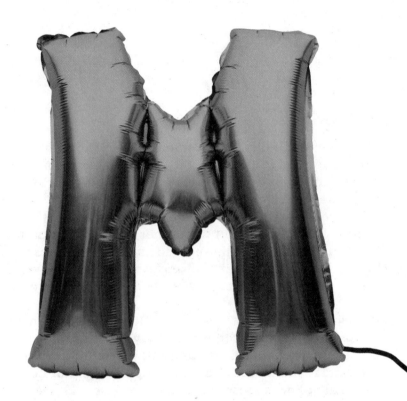

MOVEMENT

M: MOVEMENT

Movement is medicine, movement is life. Much of this book is devoted to exploring the power we have to move our thinking—from negative to positive, from guilt to gratitude, from fear to love. The moves we make in our mind are the greatest tool we have for manifesting the future of our dreams. But sometimes, moving your mind just feels impossible. The anger too fiery, the sadness too heavy, the doubt too immobilizing. And that—that is when we let go of our minds and let our bodies lead. We move.

For a long time, I resisted exercise. I loathed it. It wasn't my thing. Until I realized something: they call it working out because movement solves things. No matter how cluttered my mind is at the beginning, movement, no matter how minimal or how intense, clears me. Exercise releases endorphins that in turn shift our perception of pain. It's— quite literally—medicine.

So if you can't shake that feeling, shake that body. Chances are you'll end up feeling better—mentally, physically, emotionally, and, most of all, spiritually.

SELF LOVE
IN ACTION

Commit to dancing in your room every day this week for five minutes in the morning and five minutes before bed. It might feel silly at first, but stick with it, avoid judging yourself, and have some fun. Once you get in your flow, your body will take over. Which is exactly what you want.

Not sure which songs to play? Go back to letter H for your playlist.

Write about how your body and mind felt after some movement:

I AM NOT FOR EVERYONE. I AM FOR ME.

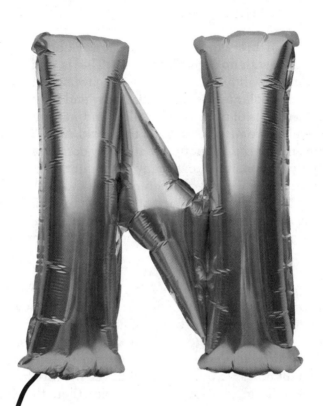

NURTURE
YOUR NATURE

N: NURTURE YOUR NATURE

Nature vs. nurture: a question we've been asking since the dawn of time with no definitive answer. That is, until now. That's right. I've figured it out. In 2012, I gave birth to twin girls who are polar opposites: Stella Avery and Violet Harper. Stella is a replica of my husband: tall, blond, naturally positive, at peace with herself and the world. And Violet is my mini-me: petite, brunette, emotionally complex, and extremely responsible. Now, many years later, they are exactly who they were at birth, completely themselves and completely the opposite of each other, despite having exactly the same environment and upbringing. They are simply becoming more vivid versions of who they were when they were born.

So the social experiment is done. It's nature. That was simple, right? Except it's not just about nature. It's about knowing and nurturing your nature and building a life that honors it, that allows you to thrive to your fullest, inherent potential. And that I suppose is where nurture comes in. As a parent, my job right now is to provide just that, the nurture to their nature. And for me, nurture is about giving them the skills to work with who they already are.

I try to nurture my nature each and every day. I strive to connect with my most authentic self and build a life that honors her. I make sure my environment and experiences are working for me instead of against me. I strive to achieve an equilibrium that honors all parts of myself. So if you're unhappy or unsettled in your life, ask yourself:
Am I nurturing my nature? Am I honoring who I am
or fighting it?

Think about who you were as a child before practicality, adulthood, competition, ego, trauma, or other external circumstances got in the way. And then nurture the hell out of your nature until you create a life that lets you be unapologetically you.

SELF LOVE
IN ACTION

Take a personality test, and get to know yourself on a deeper level. Use your findings to evaluate whether the life you've created, from the relationships you prioritize to the work you do, honors your true nature. I recommend www.16personalities.com.

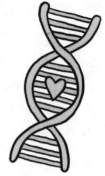

Journal about your findings below:

_____

_____

_____

_____

_____

_____

_____

_____

_____

_____

_____

_____

_____

_____

_____

_____

_____

IT WASN'T UNTIL
I CRACKED THAT
THE LIGHT WITHIN ME
POURED OUT
AND HEALED ME.

OPEN YOUR HEART

O: OPEN YOUR HEART

Think about this word: "heartbroken." You've heard it before. You've seen the emoji. A heart cracked in two. You've felt what this word embodies: pain, brokenness, irreparable harm. Let me introduce you to a new word: "heartopened." Now picture the same emoji. A heart cracked in two. But this time, instead of that being a bad thing, imagine it is a good thing. Like Leonard Cohen said, "There is a crack in everything. That's where the light comes in."

The definition of "openhearted" is helpful here. It means to be candid, to be emotionally expressive and responsive. To speak your truth is to be openhearted. To feel your feelings is to be openhearted. To receive emotion from another, you must be openhearted.

A heart opened is a heart that is able to receive. A heart opened is one that has experienced life and survived. To connect with another soul, you need an open heart. To welcome love, light, joy . . . you need an open heart. To experience the magic of vulnerability, you need an open heart. To create space for possibility, you need an open heart.

So if you're healing from a heartbreak, perhaps all you need is a shift in perspective. Instead of focusing on what happened, focus on what is now possible. Your heart is now open. Embrace the cracks, and let the light flood in.

SELF LOVE
IN ACTION

Make a list below of all the things you wish to receive: love, health, travel, commitment, community, security, intimacy, success, clarity, healing, forgiveness, strength. Now, draw these words and images to fill in the cracks of the heart on the next page. When you're feeling low, revisit your heart, and focus on the possibilities that abound for you and your open heart.

_____

_____

_____

_____

_____

_____

_____

_____

_____

_____

_____

_____

_____

_____

_____

_____

_____

_____

_____

_____

_____

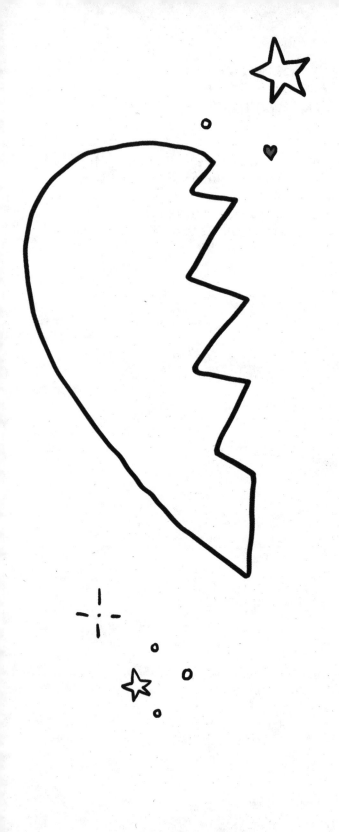

MY OPEN HEART

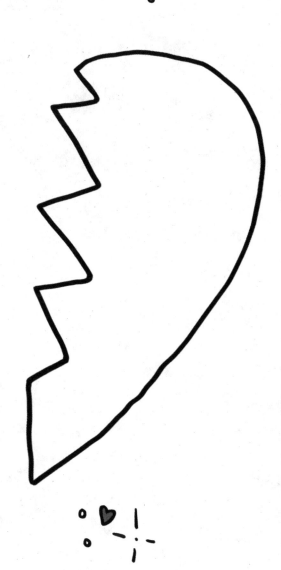

Realizing your potential is not about conquering the space between where you are and where you want to be. It is about recognizing that who you are in every moment is already ENOUGH.

PROGRESS
OVER
PERFECTION

P: PROGRESS OVER PERFECTION

"Practice makes perfect," I was told over and over, week after week. And perhaps back then, during my weekly piano lessons, there was some semblance of truth to that. I practiced and practiced and practiced, and, occasionally, my fingers would grace the keys in exactly the right sequence at exactly the right pace. I would feel high in my fleeting perfection. Of course, whatever we tell children rarely remains within a singular context. I took that notion of perfection over into all other parts of my life. In school and in my relationships with others and with myself. When it comes to human behavior, perfection is not rare. It is an impossibility. And so I disappointed others and disappointed myself. This only led me further away from my authentic self, which is the closest to perfection any of us ever get.

Now as an adult and as a mother, I've learned the power of words. The words I speak to others, to myself, and especially to my daughters. Even during piano lessons, the lesson is: "Practice makes progress," never perfection. We routinely say that perfect doesn't exist, nor is it desirable, because it is the opposite of authenticity.

I want the high they feel in life to come from trying, the journey of experience, rather than from a singular outcome. I want them to infuse their relationships with the same focus on effort, attention, and love, rather than perfection. Because when the focus is on effort rather than outcome, they do better, and they feel better along the way. And so do I. And so will you.

SELF LOVE
IN ACTION

The best way to experience the pleasure of progress is to commit to a new learning experience for thirty days. You can learn a new language, instrument, or workout or take a Photoshop or cooking tutorial. Whatever you choose, let it be something outside of your comfort zone, and try to do it every day for thirty days—even if it's only for fifteen minutes. Below, describe what you chose and how you felt along the way.

MY WORK IN PROGRESS IS: _____

_____

_____

_____

_____

_____

_____

_____

_____

_____

_____

_____

I'M MADE OF TRILLIONS OF CELLS.
I'M DONE LETTING ONE NEGATIVE
THOUGHT MAKE ALL OF
THEM SUFFER.

QUESTION
NEGATIVITY

Q: QUESTION NEGATIVITY

The most precious thing you have is your joy. Hard stop.
That's why when you encounter negativity either within
yourself or from someone else, you need to stop and question
it. Because where as challenging life events are unavoidable,
how you think and feel about them is your choice. The same
goes for everyone around you, as well.

Let me give you an example. You make dinner plans with
a friend. You both arrive at the restaurant on time.
The restaurant is running twenty minutes late. Your friend
is outraged. "Twenty minutes late? We have a reservation!
This is outrageous!" His blood is boiling. Perhaps now so
is yours. Now imagine a different scenario. You again both
show up to the restaurant that is running late on your
reservation. This time, your friend is unbothered. He smiles
at the server, says, "No problem," and then turns to you
and asks how you are doing. You spend the twenty minutes
chatting, connecting, and enjoying each other's company.
Were the circumstances different? No. But in scenario
one, negativity imbued the facts of the circumstance with
darkness. In the second, positivity imbued the facts of
the circumstance with light. Where would you rather live,
in the light or in the dark?

Choose your company carefully. If you surround yourself
with negative people, or people who make you feel negative,
negativity will prevail and seep into your soul. Once negativity
becomes your status quo, kindness, toward yourself and
toward others, is often its first causality. And without
kindness, self love is impossible.

When you encounter negativity, whether it is in your own
mind or in someone else's, ask yourself: Is this negativity
necessary? Is there another perspective I can embrace?
Sometimes the answer will be no. There are circumstances
that are so tragic that a negative response is the only one that
will suffice. Or maybe even in those circumstances, shifting
your focus to gratitude can shield you from the threat
negativity poses to your joy. Because even in the darkest
of times, there's room for gratitude. Always.

SELF LOVE
IN ACTION

Evaluate your social media accounts. Unfollow or mute accounts that elicit a negative reaction from you, even if that means disconnecting from friends or family. Unfollowing is one form of setting a boundary. Once you do it, you'll create space for something better.

Negativity on social media comes in many forms. It can be the celebrity or influencer who makes you feel less than in comparison. It can be the uncle who rages about politics. It can be the long-lost high school classmate who populates your feed with irrelevance that brings you down.

Remember: you can also disconnect with people IRL, too. Not every relationship needs to be forever. Nostalgia isn't enough of a reason to keep someone in your life if the current dynamic is a toxic one.

Write down what you let go of and what you made space for:

OLD MENTALITY:

IF I'M NOT WORKING MYSELF TO DEATH, I'M WASTING MY POTENTIAL.

NEW MENTALITY:

IF I'M NOT WORKING MYSELF TO DEATH, I'M REALIZING MY POTENTIAL.

REST

R: REST

In a culture where busyness is prized, rest is the ultimate affront. We spend the bulk of our conversations talking about everything we have to do, wearing our tightly packed schedules like a badge of honor. We fill every ounce of empty space with our phones, mindlessly scrolling through Instagram, taking pictures that will get uploaded to a cloud we'll never visit, reading articles that only reinforce our collective obsession with feeling doomed.

Rest is now a four-letter word.

It's uttered with shame when it's uttered at all. "I didn't get anything done today," we lament. And the cycle of busyness continues to spin, churning us up and spitting us out.

It's time to take back the word "rest" and all it embodies. To rest is to create space for your body to heal and your mind to wander. Science tells us that our minds need freedom from constant stimulation in order to thrive. In fact, doing nothing and also thinking about nothing are two of the greatest gifts you can give your body and mind.

It may seem counterintuitive, given our obsession with productivity, but doing nothing is the fastest way to revive yourself and actually get somewhere beyond the hamster wheel of your life. Rest, whether that means sleeping for at least eight hours, spending an afternoon at the beach or in a bath, or simply turning off your phone to take a break from its incessant command over your life, is the key to your spiritual, emotional, mental, and physical revival. Don't believe me? Give it a rest, and see how you feel.

SELF LOVE
IN ACTION

Schedule in some rest this week. The same way you'd schedule
a business meeting, workout class, or doctor appointment. Schedule
three periods of short rest (one hour or less) and two periods of long rest
(two hours or more). This is in addition to the time you spend sleeping at
night. During these periods of rest, avoid technology as much as you can,
and let your brain reset from all the digital commotion.

Remember: doing less does not make you worth less.

Zzz...
REST SCHEDULE

MONDAY: _____

TUESDAY: _____

WEDNESDAY: _____

THURSDAY: _____

FRIDAY: _____

SATURDAY: _____

SUNDAY: _____

What did you discover after adding some guilt-free, preplanned rest to your schedule?

_____

_____

_____

_____

_____

_____

_____

_____

_____

_____

_____

_____

_____

_____

_____

_____

_____

_____

_____

_____

_____

_____

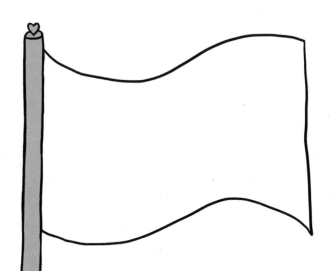

SURRENDER

ENDED THE RACE
WON THE WAR
SLOWED THE PACE
CLAIMED THE PRESENT
TOOK THE BREATH
FELT THE FEELINGS
HEALED THE WOUND
QUIETED THE MIND
OPENED THE HEART
PAVED THE WAY.

SURRENDER

S: SURRENDER

In war, surrender is a bitter, bitter thing. It happens when one side has tried absolutely everything to win and has failed, oftentimes with tragic consequences. And so it's no surprise that when we hear the word "surrender," we resist. We want to be strong. We want to win. We want to stay in control. No matter what.

But just like there are no real winners in war, there is no such thing as complete control.

I used to think that if I was strong enough, I could handle everything on my own (because alone = control). And you know what I realized? Strength based on control is actually quite fragile. Holding all the pieces together is impossible. One wrong move and everything shatters. Now I aim to be soft. To be fluid, flexible, adaptable, in harmony with my environment and those around me instead of in opposition. If strength used to come from control for me, now it comes from surrender. I've replaced my need for control with grace, trust, and curiosity and see the future as a gift to be received. I refuse to continue being at war with myself and my life. I surrender. I win.

Instead of fear for the worst or hope for the best, love yourself in every moment, and avoid being attached to a particular outcome. No longer is life about getting to point A or point B. It's about opening the door to a yet unknown point C by being part of the story instead of controlling it.

SELF LOVE
IN ACTION

When you find yourself highly committed to a specific outcome and desperate for control, ask yourself:

If the thing I want most doesn't happen, then what?

If I stop trying to make it happen, then what?

If I took the energy I'm spending worrying about tomorrow and instead focused on loving myself and my life today, then what?

THE ANSWER TO THE
QUESTIONS YOU'VE SPENT
A LIFETIME ASKING...

WILL EVERYTHING BE
OKAY, AM I OKAY, DID I DO
ENOUGH, WILL IT EVER BE
ENOUGH, WILL I FEEL IT,
THE HAPPINESS,
THE WHOLENESS,
THE PEACE, THE LOVE,
THE JOY, THE CONNECTION
I SO DEEPLY CRAVE?

YES. IF YOU ALLOW IT.

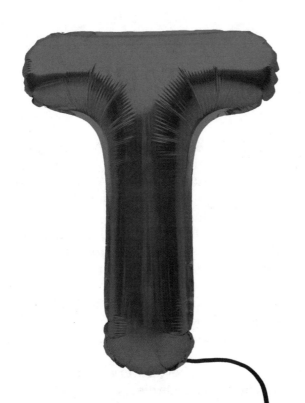

TRUST

T: TRUST

The world is simply a reflection of us. When we trust ourselves, we trust the universe. When we don't trust ourselves, we don't trust the universe. And either way, the universe listens, and the universe complies.

When you trust yourself, you start building momentum. You make choices. You make moves. You stop waiting, and the universe rewards your faith and conspires in your favor.

When you don't trust yourself and are instead indecisive or self doubting, the universe is paralyzed. Your doubt invariably makes even the right decisions wrong ones.

Imagine instead if you believed every decision you ever made was the right one. Regardless of the outcome, think about what your world would look like then.

But here's the thing: sometimes, just when you think you have it all figured out, it all falls apart. This isn't the universe testing you. You didn't make a mistake by trusting yourself or trusting the universe. This is just the universe reminding you that progress isn't linear. All is not lost. You're still on your way. Keep going.

SELF LOVE
IN ACTION

A daily gratitude practice is one way to cultivate trust. Oftentimes, when good things happen to us, we say, "I can't believe it!" because when we don't trust ourselves or the universe, our blessings feel otherworldly. Not real. Not ours. Compare this with how we treat our worries. We believe them. Boy, do we believe them. To challenge these habits, start or end each day with this gratitude practice:

I BELIEVE
[followed by all the good things you have going for you]:

_____

_____

_____

_____

_____

_____

_____

_____

_____

_____

_____

_____

_____

_____

_____

_____

_____

_____

_____

_____

I DON'T BELIEVE

[followed by all the worries or negative feelings you carry around]:

How has your life shifted now that you are practicing trust?

_____

_____

_____

_____

_____

_____

_____

_____

_____

_____

_____

_____

_____

_____

_____

_____

_____

_____

_____

_____

_____

ALL OF ME
LOVES ALL OF ME.

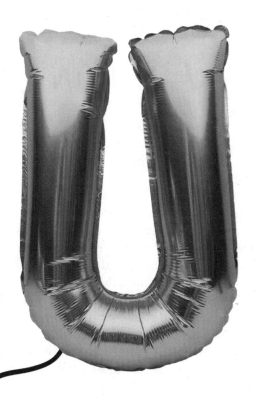

UNION

U: UNION

"Union" is a word that is most often used in the context of marriage. It is a word that symbolizes the coming together of two lives in one unbreakable bond.

Self love is when you choose to enter into union with yourself. It is a serious, lifelong commitment. Just as traditional wedding vows include "in sickness and in health" and "in good times and in bad," union requires loving yourself "in sickness and in health" and "in good times and in bad." It requires seeing and loving all parts of yourself—mind, body, and soul—including your shame, your anxiety, your creativity, your depression, your humor, your genius, your strength, your extra thirty pounds, your guilt, your anger, your mistakes, your triumphs.

When you achieve union, you no longer compartmentalize yourself. You embrace it all. You are you, in all your glory. And that is when you achieve wholeness and take ownership of your worth.

SELF LOVE
IN ACTION

Write yourself wedding vows by filling in the blanks:

Dearest _____,

I'm so proud to choose you today. You are without question the most
_____ person I know. We've been through
so much together.

I've watched with awe as you've risen to every occasion.
Your ability to _____ truly sets you apart,
and I know that with you the future will be full of _____
_____.

Thank you for teaching me _____
_____.

For being the embodiment of _____.
For always knowing what I need and giving it to me. For allowing me to
be exactly who I am in all moments.

Here are my vows to you: I promise you that I will always _____
_____ and will never _____.
As we grow together, I will remember _____
_____.

And today, tomorrow, and always, I will continue to choose you, in good
times and in bad, in sickness and in health, till death do us part.

Not everyone likes to use traditional vows.
Use this space to write your own.

GENTLE REMINDERS FOR YOUR

INNER CHILD

1 IT'S OKAY TO FEEL DEEPLY

2 IT'S OKAY TO SPEAK FREELY

3 IT'S OKAY TO THINK DIFFERENTLY

4 IT'S OKAY TO LIVE OPENLY

5 IT'S OKAY TO CHANGE FREQUENTLY

6 IT'S OKAY TO BE YOURSELF,
PROUDLY AND LOVINGLY

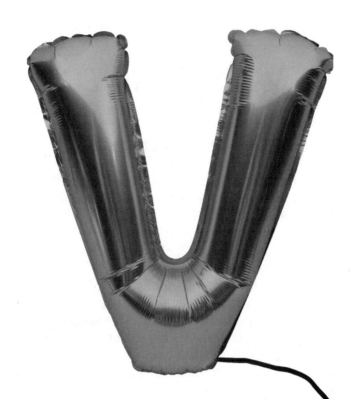

VULNERABILITY

V: VULNERABILITY

When did being yourself become difficult for you?

There was a time early on in my life when I was willing to feel anything I needed to feel, say anything I needed to say, be anyone I happened to be. I felt, spoke, and lived my truth. But as I transitioned from childhood into adolescence, it happened: my once brave inner child started to hide.

I started to relinquish my authenticity to conformity as a way to protect myself. I wanted to be liked, to fit in, to be safe. I learned to hide the parts of myself I thought were less than perfect. I stopped being willing to be true—because vulnerability meant risk: risk of being hurt, judged, and even cast out. Shame kept my vulnerability at bay for a very long time.

It takes a lot of courage to embrace vulnerability as an adult after years of hiding from it. It takes a lot of self love to choose to feel and speak and be authentic and open when we have so much to lose—especially when we're surrounded by people living picture-perfect lives (at least that's what they show us).

The thing is: once you drop the mask, the people you should keep in your life will celebrate you and follow suit. Because nothing fuels connection more than realness.
And vulnerability is as real as it gets.

SELF LOVE
IN ACTION

Write a letter from your inner child to yourself. Share the things you want to be vulnerable about, and ask for all the things you need to feel comfortable bringing those vulnerabilities to the surface.

DEAR ME,

_____

_____

_____

_____

_____

_____

_____

_____

_____

_____

_____

_____

_____

_____

I'LL LOVE
MYSELF WHOLE.

YOU LOVE
YOURSELF WHOLE.

AND WITH ALL OUR
WHOLENESS, WE WILL
LOVE EACH OTHER.

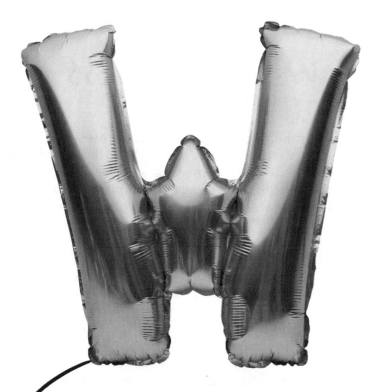

WHOLENESS

W: WHOLENESS

Once upon a time, we were sold a story. Boy meets girl, they fall in love, they are soul mates reunited, and thus, two halves make a whole. And so we learned that in order to feel whole, we need someone to come along and complete us. To love us. To choose us. And with that, we took our inherent wholeness and gave it away.

Perhaps this flawed fairy tale is the very reason why we have such a hard time embracing our whole selves. We need to be broken and incomplete in order to earn our happily ever after.

It's time we write a new story. One where self love is the foundation of all love. Where we are whole, all on our own. Where two whole-souled people come together and create something bigger than themselves through their commitments to each other and, perhaps more importantly, through their commitments to themselves. Now that's a fairy tale I could get behind.

SELF LOVE
IN ACTION

Consider the most important relationship in your life—romantic or platonic. Explore these questions to determine whether it's a whole-souled relationship.

Do you set boundaries, and are they respected?

When you're apart, do you still feel confident about the relationship?

Are you honest and showing up with integrity?

Have you grown, or do you feel stagnant in the relationship?

_____

_____

_____

_____

_____

_____

_____

_____

_____

_____

_____

_____

_____

_____

_____

_____

_____

_____

_____

_____

_____

_____

_____

Is your true self leading or another version of yourself?

HEALING MY WOUNDS INSTEAD OF HIDING THEM.

X-RAY VISION

X-RAY VISION

In comic books, superheroes like Superman use their X-ray vision to see through solid objects, like walls, to uncover the villain hiding behind them.

Imagine if you did the same but used your X-ray vision to discover the core emotion you're experiencing and, from there, what is causing it.

According to psychologist Dr. Robert Plutchik, there are eight primary emotions: joy, sadness, acceptance, disgust, fear, anger, surprise, and anticipation. Combining these emotions yields thirty-four thousand different outcomes. That's right: as humans, we are able to feel thirty-four thousand different ways. The first step toward emotional empowerment is to use your X-ray vision to uncover one of the eight core human emotions. From there, work your way out to understand the nuances of your feelings and heal their causes. You can also use this superpower to understand other people's actions and feelings.

Who or what is hiding on the other side of the wall?
Use your X-ray vision and find out.

SELF LOVE
IN ACTION

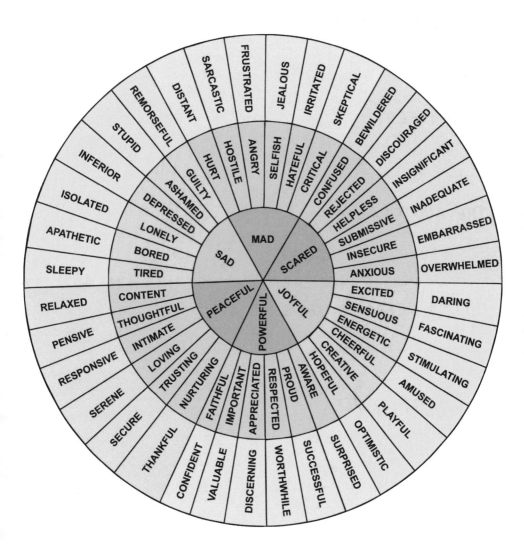

This is a variation of Gloria Wilcox's Feelings Wheel, which is an expanded expression of Plutchik's Wheel of Emotion. Start at the edge of the wheel, and put a name to your current, strongest feelings. Then trace them inward to discover their root causes.

HOW I FEEL: _____

_____

_____

THE ROOT CAUSE: _____

_____

HOW I FEEL: _____

_____

_____

THE ROOT CAUSE: _____

_____

HOW I FEEL: _____

_____

_____

THE ROOT CAUSE: _____

_____

HOW I FEEL: _____

_____

_____

THE ROOT CAUSE: _____

_____

_____

Write about what you learned when you traced your feelings, and what you plan to do next in response to your discoveries:

SELF CARE:
THE RADICAL NOTION
THAT YOU DESERVE YOUR
OWN ATTENTION.

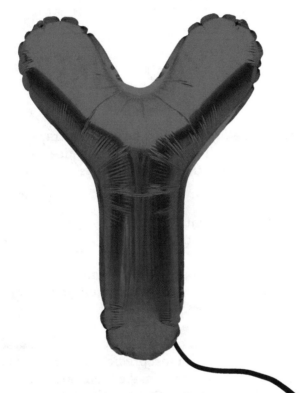

YOU FIRST

Y: YOU FIRST

Chances are the first time you heard the phrase "self love," your reaction wasn't positive. That's because we're culturally conditioned to think that self sacrifice is heroic and self care is selfish.

That. Stops. Here. Right. Now.
It's time to put you first.

Loving yourself first doesn't mean loving anyone else less. In fact, when you love and care for yourself, you're able to love others more. One begets the other.

It's time to start thinking about and caring for yourself the way you would your most precious loved one. Because ignoring your needs doesn't make them go away—it makes you, your ME, your most authentic self, go away. And running yourself into the ground only means you have less energy, love, and passion to give to the world. It's a lose-lose proposition.

So the next time you feel selfish for loving yourself or taking care of yourself first, remember that by loving yourself, you're engaging in a fierce act of rebellion against years of systematic oppression. And who doesn't want to be a rebel?

SELF LOVE
IN ACTION

Research says it takes twenty-one days to create a habit. Use this Twenty-One-Day Self Love Checklist Challenge to make connecting with your needs and putting yourself first instinctual. Do one a day in any order you please (this is all about you honoring you).

- [ ] BUY YOURSELF FLOWERS
- [ ] TREAT YOURSELF TO YOUR FAVORITE MEAL
- [ ] GO TO BED EARLY OR SLEEP IN
- [ ] WATCH AN INSPIRING TED TALK
- [ ] STICK SELF AFFIRMING NOTES TO SELF IN EVERY ROOM
- [ ] TAKE YOUR SHOES OFF AND WALK IN NATURE
- [ ] HAVE BREAKFAST WITH A FRIEND BEFORE WORK
- [ ] DO A RANDOM ACT OF KINDNESS
- [ ] TAKE TWENTY-FOUR HOURS OFF SOCIAL MEDIA
- [ ] DRESS UP EXTRA FOR A NORMAL DAY
- [ ] UNFOLLOW OR MUTE TOXIC SOCIAL MEDIA ACCOUNTS
- [ ] TAKE AN ONLINE DANCE CLASS
- [ ] SIT OUTSIDE AND READ A POETRY BOOK
- [ ] GO FOR A WALK AND LISTEN TO MUSIC
- [ ] TAKE A CANDLELIT BUBBLE BATH
- [ ] CALL OR FACETIME (DON'T TEXT) A FRIEND YOU MISS
- [ ] PUT YOUR PHONE IN ANOTHER ROOM BEFORE BED
- [ ] GIVE YOURSELF A MASSAGE (INCLUDING A HUG!)
- [ ] TAKE A TWENTY-FOUR-HOUR BREAK FROM THE NEWS
- [ ] DONATE CLOTHES THAT ARE TOO SMALL FOR YOU
- [ ] DO SOME DEEP STRETCHING BEFORE BED

Share some details about how you completed each day of this challenge:

_____

_____

_____

_____

_____

_____

_____

_____

_____

_____

_____

_____

_____

_____

_____

_____

_____

_____

_____

_____

_____

_____

_____

_____

I let go of my expectations and stopped feeling disappointed.

I stopped feeling disappointed and started feeling

ALIVE.

ZERO OUT

Z: ZERO OUT

To zero out means to remove completely. And that's exactly what I want you to do with all the uncomfortable feelings you're carrying around instead of addressing.

If it's uncomfortable, say it, feel it, do it, leave it, heal it, sooner.

Because we are not limitless. We can hold space for only so much. Let's zero out the bad by working through it and releasing it to create more space for the good. Because you deserve the good. And more of it.

For me, checking in with myself regularly started with the help of a therapist. During our weekly sessions, I would talk about what happened that week and start to discover all the feelings and thoughts I had unknowingly collected in connection with my experiences. Specifically, I learned that I had a lot of expectations. Expectations used to mean everyone around me was constantly letting me down, which in turn meant I felt alone, disappointed, and increasingly resentful. Through those weekly check-ins with my therapist, I learned to replace expectations with communication—I let people know how I feel and what I need. Now I'm grateful to regularly check in with myself. Self love, as explained throughout this book, is what allows me to know what I need and empowers me to communicate it, in real time. And it will do the same for you.

SELF LOVE
IN ACTION

In accounting, the concept of a zero-sum account is when you go through your checking account at the end of the month and allocate every dollar. Nothing is left behind. If any money isn't spent, it gets moved into a savings account. Each month, your checking starts at zero.

Now apply the same strategy to your emotional well-being. Schedule a regular accountability date with yourself—perhaps on the last weekend of every month. This is your time to feel your feelings and explore them instead of letting old feelings linger unaddressed. Zero out your emotions, and free yourself to start each month anew.

ACCOUNTABILITY DATE: _____

MY EMOTIONAL BALANCE SHEET: _____

_____

_____

_____

_____

_____

_____

_____

_____

_____

_____

CERTIFICATE OF COMPLETION

THE

ABCs

OF

SELF LOVE

PROUDLY & LOVINGLY
PRESENTED TO:

_____

YOUR NAME

_____

DATE

_____

SIGNATURE

AFTERWORD

Congratulations on completing *The ABCs of Self Love*.
I'm so proud of you. You should be, too.

Writing this book wasn't easy, primarily because there is so
much that goes into self love and there is so much more
I could have covered for each letter. B for Bravery. D for
Desire. K for Kindness.

Now that you have your initial ABCs down, I invite you to
explore yourself, and your world, to add more to your self love
vocabulary and practice.

I'd love to see a picture of your signed certificate so
I can celebrate you. Share it with me on social media
@melodygodfred with the hashtag #theabcsofselflove.

With love and gratitude, from my ME to yours,

MELODY GODFRED

ABOUT THE AUTHOR

Melody Godfred is the Self Love Philosopher. As a poet, author, and entrepreneur, she is devoted to empowering people to love themselves and transform their lives. She is the founder of global self love movement Fred and Far, creator of the Self Love Pinky Ring™, and author of *Self Love Poetry: For Thinkers & Feelers*. Her poetry has been featured by *Oprah Daily* and *TODAY with Hoda & Jenna*, among others, for its wisdom and ability to deeply resonate and uplift.

Melody lives in Los Angeles with the love of her life, Aaron; twins, Stella and Violet; and son, Teddy. Learn more at melodygodfred.com and fredandfar.com, and connect with her @melodygodfred and @fredandfar.

*this space is
for you.
please use it.*